C000161419

Diabetes Type 2

Great, Healthy, Delicious Recipes for Diabetics

By Sierra A. May

Contents

Diabetes Type 2 Cookbook

Bluesource And Friends

This book is brought to you by Bluesource And Friends, a happy book publishing company.

Our motto is **"Happiness Within Pages"**

We promise to deliver amazing value to readers with our books.

We also appreciate honest book reviews from our readers.

Connect with us on our Facebook page www.facebook.com/bluesourceandfriends and stay tuned to our latest book promotions and free giveaways.

Don't forget to claim your FREE books!

Brain Teasers:

https://tinyurl.com/karenbrainteasers

Harry Potter Trivia:

https://tinyurl.com/wizardworldtrivia

Sherlock Puzzle Book (Volume 2)

https://tinyurl.com/Sherlockpuzzlebook2

Also check out our best seller book

https://tinyurl.com/lateralthinkingpuzzles

Introduction

In *Diabetes Type 2 Cookbook: Great, Healthy, Delicious Recipes for Diabetics*, the author, Sierra A. May, proves that life with diabetes does not need to be bland or boring. With tasty recipes for breakfast, lunch, dinner, and even dessert, Ms. May proves that food can once again taste good while being good for you.

Not too many years ago, a diagnosis of Type 2 Diabetes seemed like the end of the world. Patients were cautioned to take their medicine daily and 'watch what they eat,' but the meal guidelines were somewhat vague and often conflicting. Today, with more knowledge about nutrition than ever before, it is much easier to craft delicious menus that can be eaten by the whole family.

When making these recipes, keep in mind that liquid egg and liquid egg white can be used in place of fresh eggs. Use any preferred sugar substitute in place of sugar—just follow the conversion rates on the package. Regular milk can be used in place of flavored milk. Any recipes can be made gluten-free by substituting gluten-free flour or soup for the regular kind.

While no one wants to have diabetes, it isn't the end of the world. Life does go on. And with the tips and tricks in this cookbook, life can go on even better than before.

Chapter 1: Type 2 Diabetes

Type 2 Diabetes is also known as adult-onset diabetes. With this type of diabetes, the body cannot use the insulin made by the pancreas. The pancreas makes insulin in response to food entering the body, to help the body digest the food and process the glucose in the bloodstream. Diabetes happens when the pancreas cannot produce enough insulin to keep up with the supply of glucose. The levels of glucose increase in the blood and the consequent diagnosis is Type 2 Diabetes.

Some people develop Type 2 Diabetes because they are predisposed genetically to developing certain chronic diseases. This simply means that some people will probably develop these illnesses no matter how healthy they are otherwise. There are stories all the time about the athlete being in top physical condition and suddenly dying from a heart attack or other sudden condition. People can exercise and eat healthy, but genetics cannot be changed.

There is a small gland that sits just under the stomach called the pancreas. Its job is to secrete insulin into the blood. The insulin then circulates through the body in the bloodstream. Insulin's job is to allow the cells to pick up passing sugar molecules to use for energy. So, as insulin circulates, the amount of sugar in the blood is decreased. As the sugar level drops, the pancreas begins to produce less insulin until it stops. This is in response to food being eaten. The brain signals the pancreas, which makes insulin to get the blood sugar into the cells so it can be used for energy.

But when people have Type 2 Diabetes, the process doesn't work the way it should. The sugar doesn't move into the cells as it should be. Instead, it sits in the bloodstream looking for a place to go, and usually ends up as stored fat. While the sugar is wandering around, the pancreas keeps receiving signals to make more insulin. Eventually, the pancreas stops producing properly, the body cannot keep up with the intake of sugar, and Type 2 Diabetes develops.

Besides being genetically predisposed to getting Type 2 Diabetes, lifestyle factors are the single biggest cause. Being overweight is one of these factors. When the body works at its best, food is taken in, the pancreas secretes insulin, then the insulin pushes the sugar from the food into the cells for energy, and the leftover is eliminated as waste. When people eat more food than the body really needs, they become overweight. The pancreas cannot keep up with the food intake and cannot secrete enough insulin, so it just shuts down and sends the excess sugar to be stored as fat in the body. Inactivity also plays a role, for being active helps the body to use stored sugar as energy, thus relieving some of the strain on the pancreas.

Type 2 Diabetes can be treated or sometimes cured with insulin, other oral medicines, and lifestyle changes. And lifestyle is the single biggest reason people develop Type 2 Diabetes in the first place. Being overweight and not exercising will cause diabetes. If a person takes in too much food, the body can no longer process the blood glucose with the insulin the body makes itself. This is called resistance to insulin. Lifestyle changes are important with a diagnosis of diabetes. It is quite possible to lose enough weight through exercising and following a proper diet that blood glucose levels could return to normal. The patient would then no longer be considered to be diabetic. People who develop diabetes twice are likely to have heart disease, strokes, high blood pressure, high cholesterol, and depression. A healthy lifestyle is important in the care, and possible prevention, of diabetes.

There are some myths associated with a diabetic diet that have recently been proven false. Sugar is no longer the health hazard it was once believed to be. Diabetics can enjoy desserts as long as the nutritional value is considered part of the daily diet. Just be careful to watch for sugars hidden in other foods. Carbohydrates should be limited, but are no longer off limits. And there is no need for special meals for the diabetic. As long as healthy meal plans are followed, there is no need for special foods. The entire family can eat the same meals the person with diabetes is enjoying.

There are certain food choices that should be considered when planning a diet for diabetes, though. Making good food choices is still important. Rather than thinking of food as 'good' or 'bad,' it is better to focus on eating more healthy foods and less unhealthy foods. Since overall caloric intake is so important, it is better to get those calories from highly desirable food sources. The diet plan should get its fats from avocados, flax seeds, fish oils, olive oil, and nuts. Vegetables and fruits are good, especially fresh ones, and are preferable to fruit juice. Breads and cereals should be the high-fiber variety made from whole grains. Build meals around chicken, turkey, fish, and seafood, and try to limit red meat to a few meals per week. And there are good, low-calorie options for protein, such as yogurt, low-fat dairy, beans, and eggs. Less desirable foods, those that should be avoided as often as possible, include hydrogenated fats, foods high in sugar and white flour, red meat and processed meat, low-fat foods that are high in sugar, fast foods, and prepackaged foods.

There are plenty of options for allowing sweets into the diet if good choices are made. If dessert is being served, then don't have bread with dinner. Add some nut butter or yogurt to dessert, since fat helps slow the digestion of sugars, so the levels of blood sugar don't spike as often. Have something sweet after a meal and not as a snack. And when dessert is part of the meal, take time to enjoy it. Savor each bite with good conversation over a cup of coffee or tea. Take time to savor the moment.

Don't overlook the importance of exercise when beginning this new lifestyle. Regular physical exercise will enable the body to lose weight faster. And every pound lost means being that much closer to ideal body weight and possible elimination of the need for diabetes medicine.

And if the first attempt is not successful, try again. Remember, this is a lifestyle change. No one develops this illness overnight, and no one will become healthy overnight. Keep exercising and eating a healthy diet, and the results will come.

Chapter 2: Breakfast

Breakfast has long been called the most important meal of the day, and this may be even truer for someone with diabetes. It is important to 'break the fast' that comes from hours of sleep. Fortunately, breakfast can be nutritious and can taste good while not taking a big chunk of time out of your morning.

Turkey Bacon Egg Muffins
Salmon Cream Cheese Wrap
Chocolate Overnight Oats with Almond Milk
Pumpkin Pancakes
Cottage Cheese Breakfast Bowl
Egg and Prosciutto Panini
Scrambled Eggs with Spinach and Mushrooms
Vegetable Quiche
Broccoli Turkey Casserole
Ham Egg Pitas
Southwest Scramble
Pineapple Grapefruit Smoothie
Breakfast Smoothie
Breakfast Parfait
Oatmeal Recipes

Turkey Bacon Egg Muffins

Prep time: 10 min
Cook time: 25 min
Serves 12

Great for the whole family or will keep in fridge 2 days and can be reheated in microwave.

Ingredients:

12 slices lean turkey bacon
20 egg whites (or egg white substitute)
3 eggs
2.5 oz lean turkey sausage
2.5 oz red bell pepper, chopped
2 oz spinach, chopped
3 oz yellow onion, chopped
1 clove garlic, chopped
0.5 tsp chili powder
1.5 tsp salt
1 tsp black pepper

How to make:

1. Heat oven to 350°F. Spray oil to a twelve-cup muffin pan. Place one slice of bacon in circle in each muffin form, then place chopped spinach at the bottom.
2. Sauté garlic and onion for 3 minutes, then divide between muffin cups. Add chopped bell pepper and sausage to each cup.
3. In a bowl, beat whole eggs, egg whites, pepper, and salt, then pour into muffin cups. Bake for 25 minutes.

Nutrition info per muffin:

88 calories

4.3 g fat (.5 saturated)
560 mg sodium
2.1 g carbohydrates
13 g sugar
10.8 g protein

Salmon Cream Cheese Wrap

Prep time: 10 mins
Serves 1

Ingredients:

1 8-inch flour tortilla, low carb
2 oz smoked salmon
2 tbsp cream cheese, low fat
1.5 oz red onion chopped
0.5 cup arugula or spinach
0.5 tsp basil flakes

How to make:

1. Wrap tortilla in moist paper towel and warm in microwave.
2. Mix basil and cream cheese and spread on tortilla. Add onion, arugula, and salmon. Roll, wrap, and go!

Nutrition info per serving:

291 calories
15.2 g fat (8.5 saturated)
1101 mg sodium
17.8 g carbohydrates
3 g sugar

Chocolate Overnight Oats with Almond Milk

Prep time: 5 mins
Serves 1

Ingredients:

2 oz Greek yogurt, low fat
0.7 oz oats
2 tbsp vanilla protein powder
1 tsp unsweet cocoa powder
0.5 cup almond milk
1 tsp Stevia
Slivered almonds and chopped berries if desired

How to make:

1. Blend thoroughly the milk, Stevia, cocoa, protein powder, and yogurt until smooth. Pour into container and add oats.
2. Refrigerate covered overnight. In the morning, stir and add berries and almonds if desired.

Nutrition info per serving:

183 calories
3.2 g fat (0.4 saturated)
210 mg sodium
20 g carbohydrates
3.9 g sugars
21.2 g protein

Pumpkin Pancakes

Prep time: 5 mins
Cook time: 10 mins
Serves 1

Ingredients:

0.7 oz rolled oats
3.2 oz liquid egg whites
1 oz pumpkin puree
0.5 tsp cinnamon
2 tsp Stevia
Cooking spray
Sugar-free syrup or chopped fruit as desired

How to make:

1. Mix first five ingredients until smooth.
2. Spray small pan and place over medium heat. Add batter to pan and cook 3 minutes each side. Batter will make three cakes. Top as desired.

Nutrition info:

182 calories
1.3 g fat (0 saturated)
218 mg sodium
16.1 g carbohydrates
22.6 g proteins

Cottage Cheese Breakfast Bowl

Prep time: 10 mins
Serves 1

Ingredients:

0.5 cup cottage cheese, low-fat/fat-free
0.5 cup pomegranate
0.25 cup blackberries
0.25 oz. unsweet coconut flakes
1 oz. hazelnuts

How to make:

1. Place cottage cheese in bowl. Arrange other ingredients on top.
2. If desired coconut and hazelnuts may be toasted over low heat for 3 minutes.

Nutrition info:

266 calories
14.5 g fat (6 g saturated)
387 mg sodium
18.8 g carbohydrates
17.8 g protein

Egg and Prosciutto Panini

Prep time: 30 mins
Serves 8

Ingredients:

3 large eggs
2 large egg whites
6 tbsp fat-free milk
1 green onion, thinly sliced
1 tbsp Dijon mustard
1 tbsp maple syrup
8 slices sourdough bread
8 thin slices prosciutto or deli ham
0.5 cup shredded sharp cheddar cheese
8 tsp butter

How to make:

1. Butter one side of each bread slice.
2. Beat together onion, milk, eggs, and egg whites.
3. Spray large skillet and cook mixture until set.
4. Mix syrup and mustard, then spread over four slices of bread. Top with cheese, prosciutto, and eggs.
5. Add bread slice and grill.

Nutrition info for one half sandwich:

228 calories
10 g fat (5 g saturated fat)
111 mg cholesterol
640 mg sodium
21 g carbohydrates (3 g sugars, 1 g fiber)
13 g protein

Scrambled Eggs with Spinach and Mushrooms

Prep time: 15 mins
Serves 2

Ingredients:

2 large eggs
2 egg whites
⅛ tsp salt
⅛ tsp black pepper
1 tsp butter
0.5 cup thin slice mushrooms
0.5 cup chopped spinach
2 tbsp shredded provolone cheese

How to make:

1. Beat together salt, pepper, egg whites, and eggs.
2. Warm butter in skillet over medium heat. Cook mushrooms and spinach for 4 minutes. Add egg mix and cook until set. Add cheese and stir.

Nutrition info per serving:

162 calories
11 g fat (5 g saturated)
417 mg sodium
2 g carbohydrates

Vegetable Quiche

Prep time: 15 mins
Bake time: 45 mins
Serves 6

Ingredients:

7 large egg whites, divided
2 cups cooked brown rice
1 tbsp all-purpose flour
1 cup fat-free evaporated milk
1 large egg
1 cup shredded part-skim mozzarella cheese
1 cup chopped fresh asparagus
0.5 cup fresh or frozen corn, thawed
1 jar (4-1/2 oz) sliced mushrooms, drained
0.3 cup finely chopped carrot
0.25 cup finely chopped red onion
2 tbsp minced fresh parsley
0.75 tsp dried basil
0.5 tsp salt
0.25 tsp dried oregano
2 tbsp grated Parmesan cheese

How to make:

1. Heat oven to 375°F.
2. Whisk one egg white and add rice, then mix. Spray oil 9-inch baking round. Pour rice mix into pan, and press to form on bottom and up sides.
3. Use large bowl to mix milk and flour until smooth. Mix in egg and rest of whites. Add oregano, salt, basil, parsley, onion, carrot, mushrooms, corn, asparagus, and cheese, and mix well.
4. Pour mix in baking pan and sprinkle cheese on top. Bake 45-50 minutes until set. Let it rest for 10 minutes before slicing.

Nutrition info per slice:

225 calories
5 g fat (3 saturated)
538 mg sodium
28 g carbohydrates (8 g sugar, 3 g fat)
17 g protein

Broccoli Turkey Casserole

Prep time: 20 mins
Bake time: 45 mins
Serves 6

Ingredients:

1.5 cups fat-free milk
1 can (10 3/4 oz) reduced fat and sodium condensed cream of chicken soup, undiluted
1 carton (8 oz) egg substitute
0.25 cup reduced fat sour cream
0.5 tsp pepper
0.25 tsp poultry seasoning
0.10 tsp salt
2.5 cups cubed cooked turkey breast
1 package (16 oz) frozen chopped broccoli, thawed and drained
2 cups seasoned stuffing cubes
1 cup shredded reduced-fat cheddar cheese, divided

How to make:

1. Heat oven to 350°F. Spray oil to a 9-inch by 13-inch baking dish.
2. Mix together sour cream, salt, poultry seasoning, pepper, egg substitute, soup, and milk until smooth. Add stuffing, broccoli, turkey, and half the cheese, and mix.
3. Pour into baking dish and bake 40 minutes. Add rest of cheese on top and bake 10 more minutes.

Nutrition info per serving:

303 calories
7 g fat (4 g saturated)
762 mg sodium
26 g carbohydrates (8 g sugar, 3 g fiber)

33 g proteins

Ham Egg Pitas

Prep time: 10 mins
Serves 1

Ingredients:

2 egg whites
1 egg
⅛ tsp paprika
⅛ tsp black pepper
1 slice deli ham, chopped
1 green onion, chopped
2 tbsp shredded cheddar cheese, low fat
1 whole wheat pita cut in half

How to make:

1. Scramble egg, whites, paprika, and pepper until almost set. Stir in cheese, onion, and ham, and stuff into pita halves.

Nutrition info:

323 calories
10 g fat (4 g saturated)
769 mg sodium
34 g carbohydrates (3 g sugar, 5 g fiber)
27 g protein

Southwest Scramble

Prep time: 15 mins
Serves 2

Ingredients:

4 egg whites
2 eggs
0.25 tsp pepper
2 corn tortillas cut in strips
0.25 cup fresh chopped spinach
2 tbsp low-fat shredded cheddar cheese
0.25 cup salsa

How to make:

1. In a bowl, mix eggs, whites, and pepper. Add cheese, spinach, and tortilla strips.
2. Spray oil in a skillet and scramble the eggs until set. Serve salsa on top.

Nutrition info:

195 calories
7 g fat (3 g saturated)
391 mg sodium
16 g carbohydrates (2 g sugar, 2 g fiber)
17 g protein

Pineapple Grapefruit Smoothie

Prep time: 10 mins
Serves 1

Ingredients:

1 cup coconut water
1 cup diced pineapple
1 cup baby spinach
1 small grapefruit
0.5 tsp ginger
1 cup ice

How to make:

1. Puree all ingredients in blender until smooth.

Nutrition info:

102 calories
0 g fat
3 g fiber
25 g carbohydrates
2 g protein
20 g sugar
54 mg sodium

Streusel Cinnamon Rolls

Prep time: 45 mins
Ready for: 2 hours and 45 mins
Serves 12

Ingredients:

1 cup milk + 3 tsp separate
2 tsp brown sugar
0.25 cup margarine spread
1 tsp salt
0.25 cup warm water (110 -115 degrees)
1 pack active dry yeast
1 egg beaten
4.5 cups flour
0.5 cup rolled oats
2 tsp cinnamon
0.25 cup pecans
0.5 cup light sour cream
0.25 cup powdered sugar
0.25 tsp vanilla

How to make:

1. To make the dough: Mix one cup milk, brown sugar, two tbsp margarine spread, and salt in a saucepan until warm, then set aside. Mix warm water with yeast in a large bowl, then let it stand for 10 minutes. Add milk mix and eggs to yeast mixture. Stir in with a spoon as much as you can. Knead dough on floured surface for 5 minutes. Shape into ball in greased bowl and let rise until double. Push down and rest 10 minutes. Heat oven to 375°F. Grease 9-inch by 13inch baking dish.
2. To make the streusel: Mix cinnamon with oats and the rest of the margarine spread in a bowl using fingers until crumbs form. Add pecans.

3. Roll dough ball into 0.25-inch thick rectangle. Cover with nut mix and roll into log. Make 0.75-inch thick slices. Arrange in baking dish and let rise for 30 minutes, then bake for 25 minutes.
4. While baking, mix vanilla, powdered sugar, and any remaining milk to form glaze. Dribble glaze over warm rolls and serve.

Nutrition info:

194 calories
5 g fat (1 g saturated)
3 g fiber
32 g carbohydrates,
5 g protein
5 g sugar
198 mg sodium

Breakfast Smoothie

Prep time: 5 mins
Serves 1

Ingredients:

0.5 cup plain nonfat yogurt
2 tbsp low-fat milk
0.5 cup frozen fruit, any kind

How to make:

1. Mix all the ingredients in the blender and serve.
2. Add peanut butter, cinnamon, flaxseed, kale, or spinach if desired.

Nutrition info:

170 calories
2 g fat
62 mg sodium
6 g protein
33 g carbohydrates

Breakfast Parfait

Prep time: 10 mins
Serves 1

Ingredients:

0.5 cup non-fat yogurt
0.5 cup berries any type
Chopped nuts, any variety

How to make:

1. Add all ingredients to a bowl and enjoy. Chopped berries can be strawberries, blueberries, raspberries, blackberries, etc. Chopped nuts can be almonds, cashews, walnuts, pecans, etc.

Nutrition info:

292 calories
8.8 g fat (2.6 g saturated)
172.9 mg sodium
40.2 g carbohydrates (17.4 g sugar, 6.1 g fiber)
16.7 g protein

Oatmeal Recipes

Oatmeal recipes are always a good choice for breakfast options, and this is especially true for people with Type 2 Diabetes. Oatmeal has plenty of easily digestible fiber. This will help with morning appetite control and glucose control.

Trail Mix Oatmeal
Banana Nut Oatmeal
Almond Berry Crunch Oatmeal
Peach Blueberry Oatmeal
Butterscotch Oatmeal

Trail Mix Oatmeal

Ingredients:

1 cup cooked oats
1 tsp cinnamon
2 tbsp raisins
8 chopped pecan halves
0.25 cup granola

How to make:

1. Add all ingredients to oatmeal and stir.

Nutrition info:

144 calories
9 g fiber
3 g saturated fat

Banana Nut Oatmeal

Ingredients:

1 cup skim milk
1 cup cooked oats
4 chopped walnut halves
1 small diced banana

How to make:

1. Mix walnuts and bananas to the oatmeal. Serve with a glass of skim milk.

Nutrition info:

377 calories
7 g fiber
1 g saturated fat

Almond Berry Crunch Oatmeal

Ingredients:

1 cup skim milk
1 tsp sugar substitute
1 cup cooked oats
6 chopped almond
1 cup fresh raspberries

How to make:

1. Mix almonds and raspberries into oatmeal. Serve with glass of skim milk.

Nutrition info:

395 calories
14 g fiber
1 g saturated fat

Peach Blueberry Oatmeal

Ingredients:

1 cup cooked oats
0.5 cup chopped peaches
0.25 cup blueberries
0.25 tsp vanilla
0.25 tsp cinnamon
0.25 tsp flaxseed

How to make:

1. Mix all ingredients into the hot oatmeal.

Nutrition info:

377 calories
22 g sugar
14 g fat
57 g carbohydrates
10 g fiber
11 g protein

Butterscotch Oatmeal

Ingredients:

1 cup cooked oats
0.25 cup brown sugar
0.25 tsp butter

How to make:

1. Mix all ingredients into the hot oatmeal.

Nutrition info:

357 calories
13.9 g fat
48.8 g carbohydrates
10.5 g protein
145 mg sodium

Chapter 3: Lunch Recipes

The lunch meal may require extra planning, especially when it must be taken to school or work. But with a good recipe and a little planning, healthy food can be available for any meal. These recipes either reheat well or are meant to be eaten cold, so that a good lunch option is always available.

Chicken Egg Salad
Spinach Rolls
Curry Chicken Apple Salad
Lemony Hummus
Cream Cheese and Smoked Salmon Wrap
Tuna Niçoise Salad
Turkey Meatballs
Sunshine Salad
Cheese Ham Frittata
Turkey Reuben
Roast Beef Pita
Tuna Veggie Sandwich
Thai Chicken Lettuce Wraps
Pulled Pork Sandwiches

Chicken Egg Salad

Prep time: 5 mins
Cook time: 20 mins

Ingredients:

2 cooked chicken breasts
3 hardboiled eggs
2 tbsp fat-free mayonnaise
1 tbsp curry powder
1 tbsp basil or chives (if desired)
Salt (if desired)

How to make:

1. Cook chicken by preferred method. Prepare eggs. Chop eggs and chicken into small bits. Mix with other ingredients.
2. Cool for at least 10 minutes if eating right away. Can be eaten by itself or on low-carb bread or flour tortilla.

Nutrition info:

175 calories
5.4 g fat (1.1 g saturated)
152.7 mg sodium
1.6 g carbohydrates (0.8 g fiber, 0.7 g sugar)
30.4 g protein

Spinach Rolls

Prep time: 15 mins
Cook time: 40 mins

Ingredients:

16 oz frozen spinach leaves
3 eggs
1 tbsp minced onion
2 oz finely grated carrot
1 oz low-fat mozzarella cheese
4 oz fat-free cottage cheese
0.75 cup parsley
1 clove chopped garlic
1 tsp curry powder
0.25 tsp chili powder
1 tsp salt
1 tsp pepper
Pan spray

How to make:

1. Heat oven to 400°F. Thaw spinach and mix with garlic, mozzarella, two of the eggs, and half the pepper and salt.
2. Cover baking sheet with spray oil. Put spinach mix on sheet and press flat to 0.5-inch thick. Bake for 15 minutes and cool.
3. Fry carrots, onion, and garlic for 1 minute. Add parsley, chili powder, curry, cottage cheese, the last egg, and rest of pepper and salt and then mix.
4. Spread on baked spinach. Roll carefully and bake for 25 minutes. Cool and slice.

Nutrition info:

310 calories
10.4 g fat (4.6 g saturated)

695 mg sodium
19.6 g carbohydrates (5.1 g fiber, 6.7 g sugar)
27.3 g protein

Curry Chicken Apple Salad

Prep time: 10 mins

Ingredients:

1 lb cooked and diced chicken breast
1 diced Granny Smith apple
2 stalks diced celery
2 stalks diced green onion
0.5 cup chopped cashews
1 cup nonfat plain Greek yogurt
1 tbsp tahini
4 tsp curry powder
1 tsp cinnamon

How to make:

1. Mix cinnamon, curry, tahini, and yogurt. Add other ingredients. This can be eaten by itself, on low-carb bread, or in a wrap.

Nutrition info:

326 calories
5.6 g fat (.8 g saturated)
20.3 mg sodium
8.5 g carbohydrates (1.8 g fiber, 5.1 g sugar)
28.9 g protein

Lemony Hummus

Prep time: 10 mins
Serves 4

Ingredients:

1 can drained chickpeas, save liquid
1 clove peeled garlic
2 tbsp lemon juice
0.5 tsp zest
0.25 tsp ground cumin
0.25 tsp salt
6 tbsp oil

How to make:

1. Mash chickpeas with two tablespoons liquid and salt, cumin, zest, lemon juice, and garlic. Add oil and mix well. Serve with low carb chips or veggie sticks.

Nutrition info:

16 g carbohydrates (3 g fiber)

Cream Cheese and Smoked Salmon Wrap

Prep time: 10 mins
Serves 1

Ingredients:

1 low-carb flour tortilla
2 oz smoked salmon
2 tsp low-fat cream cheese
1 tbsp minced onion
Arugula
0.5 tsp dried basil
A dash of black pepper

How to make:

1. Mix pepper, basil, and cream cheese, and spread on tortilla. Lay on onion, arugula, and salmon, and roll.

Nutrition info:

291 calories
15.2 g fat (8.5 g saturated)
1101.5 mg sodium
17.8 g carbohydrates (6.7 g fiber, 3 g sugar)
23.8 g protein

Tuna Niçoise Salad

Prep time: 10 mins
Cook time: 5 mins
Serves 1

Ingredients:

4 oz tuna
1 hardboiled egg
2 cups baby spinach
2 oz green beans
1.5 oz broccoli
1 half chopped bell pepper, red, one half chop
Cucumber, 3.25 oz.
Radish, one chop
Olives, three large black
Parsley 0.5 cup
Oil, one tsp
Balsamic vinegar, one tsp
Dijon mustard, 0.5 tsp
Pepper, 0.25 tsp

How to make:

1. Steam beans and broccoli. Lay spinach on plate. Put tuna on
   lettuce and pepper. Sprinkle on egg, cucumber, radish, and
   bell pepper. Add olives, broccoli, and beans. Blend salt,
   mustard, vinegar, parsley, and oil, and dribble over salad.

Nutrition info:

405 calories
13.1 g fat (2.5 g saturated)
586.1 mg sodium
18.4 g carbohydrates (6.2 g fiber, 8.4 g sugar)
30 g protein

Turkey Meatballs

Prep time: 15 mins
Cook time: 25 min
Serves 5

Ingredients:

Ground turkey twenty oz.
Spinach, fresh or frozen, four oz.
Oats 0.25 cup
Egg whites two
Celery two sticks
Garlic three cloves
Bell pepper, green, one half
Onion, red, one half
Parsley, 0.25 cup
Cumin, 0.25 tsp
Mustard powder, one tsp
Thyme, one tsp
Turmeric, 0.25 tsp
Chipotle pepper, 0.25 tsp
Salt, one tsp
Pepper, 0.25 tsp

How to make:

1. Heat oven to 350°F. Chop celery, garlic, parsley, spinach, green pepper, and onion fine. Add spices, oats, egg whites, and turkey, and mix. Spray oil baking sheet and place meatballs on. Bake 25 minutes.

Nutrition info:

183 calories
2.5 g fat (.6 g saturated)
582.9 g sodium

12 g carbohydrates (3.1 g fiber, 2.9 g sugar)
30.7 g protein

Sunshine Salad

Prep time: 10 mins
Serves 2

Ingredients:

Navel orange, one large peeled, halve slices
Onion, red, one quarter
Lettuce, romaine or leaf, two cups
Balsamic vinaigrette, two tbsp
Almonds, one tsp thin slice

How to make:

Place ingredients in bowl and mix with dressing.

Nutrition info:

61 calories
2.5 g fat (.3 g saturated)
1.5 g protein
108 mg sodium
9.7 g carbohydrates (2.3 g fiber, 6.2 g sugar)

Cheese Ham Frittata

Prep time: 15 mins
Bake time: 25 mins
Makes 8

Ingredients:

Eggs, six large (or egg replacer)
Egg whites, four (or egg white replacer)
Milk, fat free two tbsp
Chives, fresh minced, three tbsp
Ham, cooked, cubed, 0.75 cup
Cheddar cheese, shred one cup

How to make:

1. Heat oven to 375. Mix well salt, pepper, milk, egg whites, and eggs. Place cheese and ham in muffin cups. Pour over egg mix. Bake 20 to 25 minutes.

Nutrition info one frittata:

106 calories
4 g fat (1 g saturated)
428 mg sodium
2 g carbohydrates (1 g sugar, 0 fiber)
14 g protein

Turkey Reuben

Prep time: 25 mins
Serves 4

Ingredients:

Rye bread, eight slices
Deli turkey, thin slice, 0.5 pound
Sauerkraut, 0.5 cup rinse and drain
Swiss cheese, slice, four
Thousand Island salad dressing, 0.25 cup fat free
Butter flavored cooking spray

How to make:

1. Butter spray one side of each bread slice. Cover four slices with cheese, sauerkraut, turkey, and a drizzle of dressing. Top with remaining bread. Toast sandwiches.

Nutrition info:

310 calories
8 g fat (3 g sat)
1398 mg sodium
39 g carbohydrates (5 g fiber, 8 g sugar)
22 g protein

Roast Beef Pita

Prep time: 25 mins
Serves 3

Ingredients:

Whole wheat pita, three halves
Roast beef, deli style, .03 pound
Broccoli, fresh, 0.25 cup chop
Corn, frozen kernel, 0.25 cup thawed
Cucumber, 0.25 cup chopped
Carrots, two tbsp shred
Celery, two tbsp shred
Green onion, two tbsp chop
Horseradish, prepared 1.5 tsp
Mayonnaise, 1.5 tsp
Sour cream, low fat, 1.5 tsp
Dijon mustard, 0.5 tsp
Salt and pepper, one eighth tsp each

How to make:

1. Mix dressing ingredients. Mix onion, celery, carrot, cucumber, corn, and broccoli. Stuff pita with beef. Mix dressing mix with veggies and fill pitas. Mix without beef can be stored in fridge for next day eating.

Nutrition info for one pita:

172 calories
5 g fat (1 g saturated)
579 mg sodium
20 g carbohydrates (3 g fiber, 1 g sugar)
14 g protein

Tuna Veggie Sandwich

Prep time: 30 mins
Serves 6

Ingredients:

Onion, 0.25 cup chop
Garlic, one clove minced
Zucchini, one cup shred
Squash, yellow, one cup shred
Carrots, one cup shred
Bread crumbs, whole wheat, two cups
0.25 tsp salt
0.25 tsp pepper
Butter, one tsp
Buns, six
Cheddar cheese, low fat, six slices
Lettuce leaves, six
Tomato, six tomato

How to make:

1. Cook garlic, onion, carrots, squash, and zucchini for two minutes. Mix tuna, bread, egg, pepper, and salt. Stir in veggie mix and shape into six patties. Cook with butter five minutes each side. Serve with tomato, lettuce, and cheese on bun.

Thai Chicken Lettuce Wraps

Prep time: 35 mins
Serves 6

Ingredients:

Rice vinegar, 0.25 cup
Thai chili sauce, one tsp
Sesame oil, one tsp
Ginger, fresh, minced, two tsp
Soy sauce, one tbsp low salt
Brown sugar, one tbsp
Peanut butter, creamy, two tbsp
Mayonnaise, two tbsp low fat
Lime juice, two tbsp
Cilantro, minced, 0.5 cup
Oil, three tbsp
Garlic, one clove chopped
Peanuts, dry roasted unsalted, 0.5 cup
Carrot, shred 0.5 cup
Green onion, 0.5 cup diced
Sweet red pepper, one small dice
Chicken breast, one cup cubed
Lettuce leaves, six, leaf or bibb

How to make:

1. Put oil, cilantro, juice, mayo, peanut butter, sugar, soy sauce, ginger, sesame oil, chili sauce, and vinegar in blender, and blend smooth. Mix peanuts, carrots, onions, red peppers, and chicken. Blend dressing with chicken mix. Fill leaves. Can be stored in fridge for next day eating.

Nutrition info:

284 calories

19 g fat (2 g saturated)
222 mg sodium
12 g carbohydrates (2 g fiber, 6 g sugar)
19 g protein

Meatball Sub

Prep time: 30 mins
Cook time: 10 mins
Serves 8

Ingredients:

Basil, dried, 0.5 tsp
Oregano, dried, 0.25 tsp
Onion powder, 0.25 tsp
Garlic, two cloves minced
Onion, 0.25 cup fine chop
Bread crumbs, 0.5 cup
Egg substitute, 0.25 cup
Parmesan cheese, shredded, one cup
Mozzarella cheese, low fat two tbsp
Pasta sauce, any style two cups
Ground turkey, 1.25 pounds lean
0.25 tsp pepper
Hoagie bus, four opened

How to make:

1. Mix turkey, pepper, basil, oregano, onion powder, garlic, onion, bread, and egg substitute. Form meatballs. Cook with pan spray until browned. Pour pasta sauce over meatballs and simmer 15 minutes. Spoon onto bun and top with cheese. Mixture can be kept in fridge for 2 days.

Nutrition info:

275 calories
10 g fat (3 g saturated)
542 mg sodium
28 g carbohydrates (3 g fiber, 8 g sugar)
19 g protein

Pulled Pork Sandwiches

Prep time: 15 mins
Cook time: 7 hours
Serves 8

Ingredients:

Pork roast, 2 pounds
Cinnamon, 0.5 tsp
Cumin, 1 tsp
Chili powder, 3 tsp
Barbecue sauce, 1 cup
Onion, 1 cup chop
Tomato sauce, 8 oz can
Buns, 8

How to make:

1. Put pork in crock pot. Mix remaining ingredients (except buns) until smooth. Pour over meat. Cook low heat 7 hours. Shred meat to serves. Mix can be kept in fridge for 2 days.

Nutrition info:

322 calories
10 g fat (3 g saturated)
681 mg sodium
29 g carbohydrates (3 g fiber, 9 g sugar)
28 g proteins

Chapter 4: Dinner Recipes

There is no reason to make a separate dinner menu for somone with diabetes. All members of the family can enjoy these delicious recipes.

Cranberry Mustard Pork Medallions

Prep time: 15 mins
Cook time: 20 mins
Serves 4

Ingredients:

Cranberries, dried, 0.3 cup
Dijon mustard, three tbsp
Butter, 1 tbsp
Oil, 1 tbsp
Pepper, 0.25 tsp
Garlic salt, 0.25 tsp
Pork tenderloin, 1 pound
Cranberry juice, 0.5 cup thawed concentrate
Apple juice, thawed concentrate 0.25 cup
Water, 0.5 cup

How to make:

1. Mix water and juices. Slice pork into one-half inch medallions
    and fry 3 minutes each side. Pour juice mix in skillet and add
    cranberries and mustard. Simmer 10 minutes.

Nutrition info:

332 calories
11 g fat (4 g saturated)
419 mg sodium
34 g carbohydrates (1 g fiber, 27 g sugar)
23 g proteins

Ravioli with Snap Peas and Mushrooms

Prep time: 30 mins
Serves 8

Ingredients:

Hazelnuts, 0.25 cup chop
Parmesan cheese, shred 0.25 cup
White pepper, 0.25 cup
Lemon pepper season, 1 tsp
Lemon zest, 1 tsp
Sage, rubbed 2 tsp
Evaporated milk, fat free 2cups
Garlic, 2 cloves minced
Shallots, 3 fine chops
Mushrooms, fresh 0.5 pound
Butter, 1 tbsp
Sugar snap peas, 1 pound
Cheese ravioli, 20 oz package

How to make:

1. Use package directions to cook ravioli. Add peas last 3
   minutes, then drain. Cook garlic, shallots, and mushrooms in
   butter five minutes. Add white pepper, lemon pepper, zest,
   sage, and milk, and boil. Simmer 3 minutes. Pour sauce over
   ravioli mix, and serve garnished with cheese and hazelnuts.

Nutrition info:

347 calories
11 g fat (5 g saturated)
470 mg sodium
44 g carbohydrates (4 g fiber, 11 g sugar)
20 g protein

Cheesy Spinach Stuffed Shells

Prep time: 45 mins
Serves 12

Ingredients:

Marinara sauce, 1 jar twenty four oz
Mozzarella cheese, 1.5 cups low fat divide
Italian cheese blend, 1.5 cups divide
Black olives, 1 can 4.25 oz.
Pepper, 0.25 tsp
Spinach, 10-oz package thawed and dried
Ricotta cheese, 15 oz low fat
Eggs, 2 beaten
Garlic, 2 cloves minced
Onion, 1 small chop fine
Mushrooms, 1 cup sliced
Butter, 1 tbsp
Pasta shells, jumbo, 12 oz.

How to make:

1. Heat oven to 375. Cook pasta al dente by pack instructions. Drain and rinse. Fry garlic, onion, and mushroom in butter. Mix pepper, basil, spinach, ricotta cheese, and eggs. Add 1 cup sauce to 9-inch by 13-inch dish. Stuff cheese mix in pasta, place in dish. Cover with remaining sauce. Bake 45 minutes. Cover with cheeses and stand 5 minutes.

Nutrition info for three shells:

313 calories
13 g fat (7 g saturated)
642 mg sodium
32 g carbohydrates (3 g fiber, 5 g sugar)
18 g protein

Diabetes Type 2 Cookbook

Pot Roast with Veggies

Prep time: 10 mins
Bake time: 2.5 hours
Serves 8

Ingredients:

Chuck pot roast, boneless 3 pounds
Cornstarch, two tsp
Leeks, 3 small cubes
Parsnips, 4 medium cubed
Carrots, 4 medium cubed
Potatoes, 16 new halve
0.75 cup water + 1 tbsp divide
Oil, 1 tbsp
Lemon pepper season, 0.25 tsp
Oregano, 1 tsp
Garlic, 1 clove minced

How to make:

1. Brown roast 5 minutes. Mix lemon pepper, oregano, and garlic; add to roast in pot. Pour in 0.75 cup water. Simmer 1.5 hours. Add cornstarch and water to pan drippings to make gravy.

Nutrition info:

287 calories
7 g fat (0 g saturated)
48 mg sodium
28 g carbohydrates (0 fiber 0 sugar)
27 g protein

Mushroom Beef Skillet

Prep time: 30 mins
Serves 4

Ingredients:

12 oz cooked egg noodles
0.5 tsp garlic powder
1 tsp prepared mustard
1 tsp paprika
0.5 cup plain fat-free yogurt
0.25 cup water
2 tbsp cornstarch
2 tbsp flour
1 large chopped onion
1 lb sliced fresh mushrooms
2 cups low-sodium beef broth
1 lb beef flank steak

How to make:

1. Brown beef in skillet for 5 minutes each side and remove. Add onion, mushrooms, and broth to skillet, then cook for 5 minutes.
2. Blend water, cornstarch, and flour to make a slurry, then pour into the broth. Boil for 2 minutes.
3. Mix garlic powder, mustard, paprika, and yogurt, and add to broth mix. Cut the beef into thin slices and add to broth. Pour over hot noodles.

Nutrition info:

264 calories
9 g fat (4 g saturated)
325 mg sodium
18 g carbohydrates (2 g fiber, 6 g sugar)

28 g protein

Baked Fish and Veggies

Prep time: 25 mins
Serves 1

This recipe is easy to increase for additional servings.

Ingredients:

1 6-oz halibut steak
0.25 tsp crushed pepper
0.25 cup Sprite Zero
Half sliced medium green pepper
2 lemon slices
3 sliced cherry tomatoes
4 sliced mushrooms

How to make:

1. Heat oven to 375°F. Tear a 14-inch by 12-inch piece of foil. Lay veggies on top of fish and fold foil up. Pour Sprite over all. Seal the foil. Bake in pan for 25 minutes. Season with pepper.

Nutrition info:

205 calories
4 g fat (0 sat)
95 mg sodium
8 g carbohydrates (no sugar or fiber)
34 g protein

Asian Pork Chops

Prep time: 10 mins + another 10 mins for marinate/grill
Serves 4

Ingredients:

4 boneless 0.5-inch thick pork loin chops
0.5 tsp ground ginger
3 cloves minced garlic
1 tbsp oil
1 tbsp lemon juice
3 tbsp honey

How to make:

1. Mix liquids and spices, then add the chops. Marinate in fridge for 4 to 8 hours.
2. Broil or grill the chops for 5 minutes each side.

Nutrition info:

225 calories
9 g fat (0 sat)
420 mg sodium
16 g carbohydrates (no sugar or fiber)
21 g protein

Herbed Chicken

Prep time: 15 mins
Bake time: 70 mins
Serves 4

Ingredients:

4 to 5 lb chicken pieces
2 cubed carrots
2 cubed medium onion
1 lb peeled and laved potatoes
2 bay leaves
0.5 tsp crushed dried rosemary
0.25 tsp thyme
1 tbsp chicken bouillon granules
1 cup water

How to make:

1. Heat oven to 350°F. Mix bay leaves, rosemary, thyme, bouillon, and water. Place chicken, carrots, onions, and potatoes in baking pan. Pour juice over all. Bake covered for 1 hour, then bake uncovered for 30 minutes more.

Nutrition info:

213 calories
4 g fat (0 sat)
89 mg sodium
20 g carbohydrates (0 sugar or fiber)
24 g protein

Chicken Angelo

Prep time: 15 mins
Bake time: 30 mins
Serves 4

Ingredients:

4 skinless boneless chicken breast
Hot cooked noodles or rice
0.75 cup chicken broth
Chopped parsley
6 slices low-fat mozzarella cheese
2 tbsp butter
1 cup bread crumbs
0.5 cup egg substitute
0.5 lb fresh mushrooms, divide

How to make:

1. Heat oven to 350°F. Pour half of mushrooms in the baking dish.
2. Coat chicken with egg, then roll in the crumbs. Brown in butter 5 minutes each side. Lay chicken on top of mushrooms, then pour on remaining mushrooms, cheese, and broth. Bake for 35 minutes. Garnish with parsley.

Nutrition info:

482 calories
26 g fat (0 saturated)
695 mg sodium
25 g carbohydrates (0 fiber and sugar)
45 g protein

Cod with Tomato Sauce

Prep time: 30 mins
Serves 4

Ingredients:

Hot cooked pasta or rice, if desired
0.25 tsp red pepper flakes
0.25 tsp black pepper
0.25 tsp dried oregano
2 thinly sliced medium onions
2 tbsp oil, divide
4 6-oz cod fillets
2 cans 14-15 oz diced tomatoes with seasonings, do not drain

How to make:

1. Puree tomatoes.
2. Fry fish for 4 minutes each side and set aside. Add pureed tomatoes, seasonings, and onions, and boil. Return cod and simmer for 10 minutes.

Nutrition info:

271 calories
8 g fat (1 g saturated)
746 mg sodium
17 g carbohydrates (4 g fiber, 9 g sugar)
29 g protein

Vegetarian Chili

Prep time: 15 mins
Serves 16

Ingredients:

0.25 tbsp garlic powder
1.5 tbsp dried basil
1.5 tbsp oregano
1 tbsp cumin
1 can whole corn kernel corn
1 can pinto beans
1 can kidney beans
1 can black beans
1 can chopped tomatoes
1.5 cups mushrooms
2 tbsp chili powder
1 cup chopped red bell pepper
1 cup chopped green bell pepper
1 cup chopped carrots
1 cup chopped onion
3 cloves minced garlic
1 tbsp oil

How to make:

1. In a soup pot, cook peppers, carrots, onion, and garlic in oil for 5 minutes, stirring often. Add chili powder. Add remaining ingredients and boil. Simmer on low heat 30 minutes, stirring often.

Nutrition info:

98 calories
1.8 g fat
4.4 g protein

18.5 g carbohydrates (5.1 g fiber)
278 mg sodium

Ham Soup

Prep time: 1 hour
Serves 10

Ingredients:

1 cup low-fat cream
0.3 cup flour
0.5 cup water
5 chopped green onions
2 stalks chopped celery
4 cups chopped cabbage
5 chopped potatoes
3 cups cubed cooked ham
3 quarts vegetable broth

How to make:

1. Boil all ingredients in large pot. Lower heat and simmer for 1 hour.

Nutrition info:

111 calories
0.2 g fat (0 sat)
33 mg sodium
24.8 g carbohydrates (3.7 g fiber, 2 g sugar)
3.3 g protein

Turkey Tetrazzini

Prep time: 40 mins
Serves 6

Ingredients:

2 tbsp parsley
0.25 cup shredded Parmesan cheese
1 cup chopped cooked turkey breast
0.25 tsp nutmeg
0.25 tsp black pepper
0.5 tsp chicken bouillon granules
1 12-pz can fat-free evaporated milk
3 tbsp flour
0.5 cup water
0.75 cup chopped sweet pepper, red or green
2 cups sliced fresh mushrooms
4 oz dried whole wheat spaghetti

How to make:

1. Heat oven to 400°F.
2. Use package instructions to cook spaghetti. Drain.
3. Cook sweet pepper and mushrooms for 5 minutes. Blend
   flour and water, then add to veggie mix. Mix in nutmeg,
   pepper, bouillon, and milk until thick, stir often. Add
   spaghetti, parsley, parmesan, and turkey. Bake for 20 minutes.

Cauliflower Shrimp Bake

Prep time: 15 mins
Bake time: 40 mins
Serves 4

Ingredients:

1 tbsp chopped fresh dill
0.5 cup crumbled low-fat feta cheese
1 tsp lemon zest
2 cloves minced garlic
2 cans no-salt diced tomatoes
1 lb frozen or fresh peeled shrimp
0.25 tsp salt
0.25 tsp crushed red pepper
2 tbsp oil
5 cup chopped onion
4 cups small cauliflower florets

How to make:

1. Heat oven to 425°F. Mix salt, red pepper, oil, onion, and cauliflower, then bake for 25 minutes.
2. Mix zest, garlic, tomatoes, and shrimp, and pour over cauliflower mix, then bake for 15 minutes. Cover with dill and cheese.

Turkey Zucchini Lasagna

Prep time: 1 hour
Bake time: 1 hour
Serves 6

Ingredients:

2 tbsp shredded mozzarella cheese
3 large zucchini
2 tbsp chopped fresh basil
0.25 tsp nutmeg
1 egg white
0.75 cup fat-free cottage cheese
28-oz can crushed tomatoes
3 tbsp tomato paste
1 tsp oregano
1 tbsp minced garlic
0.5 cup shredded carrot
1 chopped medium onion
1 tbsp oil
0.25 tsp crushed red pepper
1 lb ground turkey

How to make:

1. Heat oven to 350°F. Mix turkey with onion, red pepper, brown. Add carrot, oregano, and garlic and cook 5 minutes. Mix in tomatoes and paste, then simmer 10 minutes. Mix nutmeg, egg white, basil, mozzarella cheese, and cottage cheese.
2. Cut long slices of zucchini and drop in boiling water. Boil for 5 minutes and drain.
3. Layer zucchini strips with sauce mix and cheese mix in baking dish. Bake for 1.5 hours. Cover with mozzarella cheese.

Chapter 5: Salad Recipes

It is important to eat regular meals, but sometimes at the end of the day a simple meal is the best.

Grilled Tenderloin Salad
Greek Salad
Quick Niçoise Salad
Ham and Fruit Salad
Barley Veggie Salad
Tuna Mediterranean Salad
Salmon Couscous Salad
Seafood Salad with Ginger Dressing
Taco Salad
Quinoa and Black Bean Salad

Grilled Tenderloin Salad

Prep time: 30 mins
Serves 5

Ingredients:

Salad
1 lb pork tenderloin
2 cubed sectioned seedless oranges
2 cups mixed salad greens
Dressing
2 tsp Dijon mustard
2 tsp honey
1 tbsp orange zest
2 tbsp cider vinegar
2 tbsp oil
0.5 cup orange juice

How to make:

1. Mix dressing ingredients, then chill.
2. Cook tenderloin in skillet for about 10 minutes per side, then slice thinly. Place slices on salad mix and top with dressing.

Nutrition info:

211 calories
9 g fat (2 g saturated)
113 mg sodium
13 g carbohydrates (3 g fiber, 8 g sugar)
20 g protein

Greek Salad

Prep time: 25 mins
Serves 2

Ingredients:

Leaf lettuce, two cups chopped
Salt, 0.10 tsp
Sugar, 0.25 tsp
Garlic, 1 clove minced
Oil, 2 tsp
Water, 2 tsp
Red wine vinegar, 1 tbsp
Feta cheese, 1 tbsp crumble
Black olives, 2 tbsp slice
Red onion, 1 cut in quarters
Radishes, 2 sliced thinly
Cucumber, 4 slices cut in half
Tomato, 1 small in wedges

How to make:

1. Combine all ingredients and split between two bowls, or eat half and save the other half for the next day's lunch.

Nutrition info:

89 calories
46 g fat (1 g saturated)
265 mg sodium
7 g carbohydrates (2 g fiber, 3 g sugar)
2 g protein

Quick Niçoise Salad

Prep time: 25 minutes
Serves 4

Ingredients:

2 chopped medium-sized tomatoes
3 pouches or 1 6-oz can tuna in water, divided
4 large sliced hardboiled eggs
6 cups chopped Romaine lettuce
0.25 tsp black pepper
0.25 tsp lemon zest
0.5 cup oil and vinegar salad dressing
0.25 lb trimmed fresh green beans
2 large cubed red potatoes

How to make:

1. Boil beans and potatoes for 10 minutes. Let it cool.
2. Mix lemon zest and pepper with dressing.
3. Lay romaine on plates, cover with tomatoes, tuna, eggs, green beans, and potatoes. Serve dressing on side.

Nutrition info:

327 calories
15 g fat (2 g saturated)
691 mg sodium
27 g carbohydrates (5 g fiber, 7 g sugar)
21 g protein

Ham and Fruit Salad

Prep time: 25 mins
Chill time: 1 hour
Serves 4

Ingredients:

1 small wedged melon, honeydew, or cantaloupe
0.25 tsp curry powder
1 tbsp milk
0.5 cup mayonnaise
0.5 cup sliced celery
2 medium cubed apples
1.5 cups cooked ham
0.25 cup chopped pecans

How to make:

1. Mix curry powder, milk, and mayo in bowl. In another bowl, mix the celery, apples, and ham. Pour mayo mix over ham mix and stir together. Chill for 1 hour. Add chopped pecans. Serve with sides of melon wedges.

Nutrition info:

181 calories
3 g fat (0 sat)
987 mg sodium
27 g carbohydrates (no fiber or sugar)
12 g protein

Barley Veggie Salad

Prep time: 30 mins
Chill time: 1 hour
Serves 6

Ingredients:

Salad
2 tbsp minced fresh parsley
1 small chopped sweet yellow pepper
1 small thinly sliced halved zucchini
1 medium chopped tomato
1 cup quick cook barley
0.75 cup water
1.25 cup low-salt chicken or vegetable broth

Dressing
0.25 cup almond slivers
0.25 tsp pepper
0.5 tsp salt
1 tbsp minced fresh basil
1 tbsp lemon juice
1 tbsp water
2 tbsp white wine vinegar
3 tbsp oil

How to make:

1. Bring barley to boil with water. Simmer for 10 minutes, then set aside.
2. Mix dressing ingredients, then mix barley, parsley, zucchini, yellow pepper, and tomato, coat with dressing and chill for 3 hours. Sprinkle some almonds before serving.

Nutrition info per 0.75 cup:

211 calories
10 g fat (1 g saturated)
334 mg sodium
27 g carbohydrates (7 g fiber 2 g sugar)
6 g protein

Tuna Mediterranean Salad

Prep time: 25 mins
Serves 4

Ingredients:

0.5 cup feta cheese
4 cups chopped lettuce
5-oz can white tuna in water, drained
0.25 tsp pepper
0.25 tsp salt
0.5 tsp dried basil
2 tbsp spicy brown mustard
2 tbsp balsamic vinegar
2 tbsp oil
4 chopped green onions
2 small chopped sweet red pepper
3 chopped celery
15-oz can chickpeas, drained and rinsed

How to make:

1. Blend basil, salt, pepper, mustard, vinegar, and oil. Mix green onion, red pepper, celery, and beans, and pour dressing mix over. Add tuna and stir. Spoon onto lettuce and garnish with feta cheese.

Nutrition info per 1.5 cup:

282 calories
11 g fat (2 g saturated)
682 mg sodium
23 g carbohydrates (6 g fiber, 6 g sugar)
23 g protein

Salmon Couscous Salad

Prep time: 10 mins
Serves 1

Great for leftover salmon.

Ingredients:

2 tbsp feta cheese
0.25 cup sliced dried apricots
4 0z cooked salmon
0.25 cup cooked couscous
2 tbsp white wine vinaigrette
3 cups baby spinach
0.25 cup diced eggplant
0.25 cup sliced mushroom button

How to make:

1. Brown mushrooms and eggplant for 5 minutes.
2. Mix one tablespoon of vinaigrette with spinach and put on plate. Mix couscous with rest of vinaigrette and spoon on top of the spinach. Lay salmon on couscous. Cover with feta cheese, apricots, and veggies.

Nutrition info per cup:

464 calories
22 g fat (5 g saturated)
35 g carbohydrates (6 g fiber, 0 sugar)
352 mg sodium
35 g protein

Seafood Salad with Ginger Dressing

Prep time: 20 mins
Serves 6

Ingredients:

1 lb frozen or fresh sea scallops, cooked and chilled
8 oz deveined and peeled shrimp, cooked and chilled
Chopped nuts, almonds, or cashews
2 large cleaned and chunked mango
6 cups mixed salad greens
1 tbsp orange juice
0.5 tsp orange zest
1 tsp white wine vinegar
0.5 tsp ground ginger
0.3 cup low-fat sour cream

How to make:

1. Mix together the orange juice, zest, vinegar, ginger, and sour cream to make the dressing.
2. Mix mango, spinach, shrimp, and scallops. Pour dressing over and mix.
3. Place lettuce on plates and top with seafood mix. Garnish with cashews.

Nutrition info:

194 calories
5 g fat (1 g saturated)
16 g carbohydrates (2 g fiber, 11 g sugar)
206 mg sodium
23 g protein

Taco Salad

Prep time: 30 mins
Serves 4 to 6

Ingredients:

2 cups salsa
6 cups shredded lettuce
1 medium bag crushed tortilla chips
1 cup shredded cheddar cheese
1 taco season packet
1 sliced red onion
1 grated carrot
1 cup diced tomato
1 lb cooked and drained ground beef

How to make:

1. Mix beef with taco season using package instructions. Mix onion, cheese, tomato, carrots, and lettuce. Add taco meat and chips. Garnish with salsa.

Nutrition info:

330 calories
7 g fat (1.5 g saturated)
45 g carbohydrates (8 g fiber)
580 mg sodium
21 g protein

Quinoa and Black Bean Salad

Prep time: 1 hour
Serves 2 to 3

Ingredients:

1.5 cup cooked quinoa
0.3 cup oil
1.25 tsp cumin
1 tsp salt
5 tbsp lime juice
2 diced jalapeno peppers
0.75 cup chopped bell pepper
15 tbsp red wine vinegar
1.5 cup whole corn kernel
1 15-oz drained and rinsed black beans

How to make:

1. To make the dressing, mix oil, cumin, salt, and lime juice and blend well. Mix remaining ingredients. Pour dressing over mix and stir. Refrigerate for 30 minutes.

Nutrition info:

170 calories
6 g fat (1 g saturated)
190 mg sodium
26 g carbohydrates (4 g fiber)
5 g protein

Chapter 6: Desserts

Baked Apples

Prep time: 30 mins
Serves 4

Ingredients:

1.5 cups orange juice
0.5 tsp cinnamon
4 cored apples
4 tsp sugar-free strawberry jam

How to make:

1. Heat oven to 400°F. Spoon jam in each apple and sprinkle on cinnamon. Pour juice into pan. Baked for 25 minutes.

Nutrition info:

126 calories
0 fat
1 mg sodium
36 g carbohydrates (0 fiber or sugar)
1 g protein

Raspberry Angel Cake

Prep time: 15 mins
Cook time: 45 mins
Serves 12

Ingredients:

1 tbsp sugar
0.5 tsp vanilla
0.5 tsp almond extract
1 angel food cake mix
0.3-oz package sugar-free raspberry gelatin
12-oz frozen raspberries, thawed

How to make:

1. Use package instructions to mix cake. Add extracts and blend. Pour the 0.66 of batter into an angel cake pan.
2. Mix gelatin with rest of batter. Pour the batter in a baking pan and swirl with knife. Use package instructions for baking. Cool for one hour. Slice and garnish with raspberries.

Nutrition info:

155 calories
0 fat
224 mg sodium
35 g carbohydrates (1 g fiber, 25 g sugar)
4 g protein

Almond Cheesecake Bars

Prep time: 20 mins
Bake time: 35 mins
Makes 3 dozens

Ingredients:

Cookie
0.5 cup powdered sugar
1 cup room temperature butter
2 cups flour

Filling
2 beaten eggs
1 tsp almond extract
0.5 cup sugar
8 oz room temperature cream cheese
Frosting
5 tsp milk
1 tsp almond extract
0.25 cup room temperature butter
1.5 cups powdered sugar

How to make:

1. Heat oven to 350°F. Mix cookie ingredients and cover bottom of 9-inch by 13-inch baking dish. Bake for 20 minutes.
2. Mix filling ingredients and pour over cooled cookies. Bake for 15 minutes.
3. Mix frosting ingredients and cover the cookies. Keep refrigerated.

Nutrition info per bar:

145 calories

9 g fat (5 g saturated)
68 mg sodium
15 g carbohydrates (0 fiber, 9 g sugar)
2 g protein

Lemon Pound Cake

Prep time: 20 mins
Bake time: 50 mins
Serves 16

Ingredients:

1 cup fat-free vanilla Greek yogurt
0.5 tsp salt
2.5 tsp baking powder
1.5 cups flour
1 tsp vanilla extract
2 tsp lemon zest
2 tbsp lemon juice
2 eggs
0.75 cup sugar
0.25 cup room temperature butter

How to make:

1. Heat oven to 350°F. Spray oil on the loaf pan.
2. Cream eggs, sugar, and butter. Mix in vanilla, zest, lemon juice, and oil to the cream mix.
3. Mix in salt, baking powder, and flour.
4. Add yogurt to cream mix and then add dry ingredients, mix until smooth. Pour into baking pan. Bake for 50 to 60 minutes. Cool for 10 minutes, then remove from the pan.

Nutrition info:

145 calories
6 g fat (2 g saturated)
253 mg sodium
20 g carbohydrates (0 fiber, 11 g sugar)
4 g protein

Chocolate Cream Delight

Prep time: 30 mins
Chill time: 1 hour
Serves 9

Ingredients:

2 cups low-fat whipped topping
3 oz low-fat cubed cream cheese
3.5 cups fat-free milk
2 packs sugar-free, cook-and-serve chocolate pudding mix
2 tbsp melted butter
1 tbsp sugar
1 cup chocolate wafer crumbs

How to make:

1. Mix butter, sugar, and crumbs, and press in the bottom of an 8-inch square dish.
2. Mix milk and pudding and boil, then remove from heat.
3. Pour half of the pudding over the crust. Add remaining pudding mix to cream cheese and mix until smooth. Spread gently on pudding layer. Chill for 2 hours. Before serving, spread with whip topping.

Nutrition info per serving:

211 calories
10 g fat (6 g saturated)
276 mg sodium
25 g carbohydrates (1 g fiber, 8 g sugar)
6 g protein

Cherry Spice Rice Pudding

Prep time: 10 mins
Cook time: 2 hours
Serves 12

Ingredients:

0.25 tsp ground nutmeg
0.5 tsp ground cinnamon
2 tsp vanilla
3 tbsp room temperature butter
0.75 cup dried cherries
0.25 cup water
0.3 cup sugar
1 cup low-fat milk
1 12-oz can evaporated milk
4 cups cooked long grain rice

How to make:

1. Mix all the ingredients and spoon into the crock pot. Cook low for 2 to 3 hours until mix is thick.

Nutrition info per half cup serving:

193 calories
5 g fat (4 g saturated)
61 mg sodium
31 g carbohydrates (0 fiber, 15 g sugar)
4 g protein

Gingerbread Biscotti

Prep time: 25 mins
Bake: 40 mins
Makes 48 slices

Ingredients:

0.25 tsp nutmeg
0.25 tsp ground cloves
0.75 tsp ground cinnamon
1.5 tbsp ground ginger
1 tbsp baking powder
1 cup whole wheat flour
2.25 cups all-purpose flour
0.25 cup molasses
3 eggs
1 cup white sugar
0.3 cup oil

How to make:

1. Heat oven to 375°F.
2. Mix molasses, eggs, sugar, and oil, then mix the dry ingredients and spices. Combine wet and dry mix, then stir until dough ball forms.
3. Make two dough balls and roll into logs as long as the baking sheet. Place them on greased sheet and pat to 1.5-inch thick. Bake for 25 minutes. When cool, cut in 0.5-inch thick slices. Return slices to sheet and bake for 5 minutes.

Nutrition info per slice:

70 calories
2 g fat (0 sat)
12.1 g carbohydrates (.6 g fiber, 5 g sugar)
26 mg sodium

1.4 g protein

Banana Oat Bars

Prep time: 5 mins
Bake time: 35 mins
Serves 18

Ingredients:

1 tsp vanilla extract
2 egg whites
0.25 cup skim milk
1 cup mashed bananas
0.5 cup raisins
0.5 tsp baking soda
1 tsp cinnamon
2 tsp baking powder
0.5 cup sugar
1.3 cups quick cook oats

How to make:

1. Heat oven to 350°F. Cream vanilla, milk, egg whites, and bananas.
2. In separate bowl, mix all the remaining ingredients. Add in the creamed mix and mix until smooth.
3. Spray oil on a 9-inch x 13-inch baking dish and spread cookie mixture to all sides. Bake for 35 minutes. Cool before cutting.

Nutrition info per bar:

72 calories
0.5 g fat (0 sat)
98 mg sodium
16.1 g carbohydrates (1.1 g fiber, 10 g sugar)
1.6 g protein

Sugarless Applesauce Cake

Prep time: 10 mins
Bake time: 1 hour
Serves 12

Ingredients:

0.5 cup raisins
1 tsp vanilla
2 eggs
0.75 cup brown sugar twin
1.5 cup unsweetened applesauce
0.5 tsp salt
0.5 tsp nutmeg
0.5 tsp cinnamon
1 tsp baking soda
1 tsp baking powder
2 cups flour

How to make:

1. Heat oven to 350°F. Spray oil in a loaf oven pan.
2. Sift together dry ingredients. Cream vanilla, applesauce, sugar twin, and eggs until smooth. Mix with dry ingredients and add raisins. Spoon batter into baking dish. Bake for 1 hour.

Nutrition info per slice:

125 calories
1.1 g fat (0 sat)
263 mg sodium
25.6 g carbohydrates (1.2 g fiber, 8 g sugar)
3.4 g protein.

Chocolate Brownies

Prep time: 10 mins
Bake time: 25 mins
Serves 16

Ingredients:

1 cup white sugar
1 tsp baking powder
2 egg whites
0.5 cup applesauce
3 tbsp chocolate syrup
0.25 cup unsweetened cocoa powder
0.5 cup cake flour
1 cup all-purpose flour

How to make:

1. Heat oven to 325°F. Cream wet ingredients, then stir in the dry ingredients until smooth. Spoon mix into a 9-inch by 13-inch baking pan. Bake for 20-25 minutes.

Chapter 7: Breads

There are days when fresh warm bread makes everything better!

Banana Coconut Bread
Feta and Onion Scones
Vegan Cornbread
Tomato Artichoke Focaccia
Rhubarb Oat Muffins
Sesame Cheese Twist
Lemon Bread
Cheddar Biscuits
Pizza Crust

Banana Coconut Bread

Prep time: 30 mins
Bake time: 1 hour
Serves 12

Ingredients:

0.25 cup shredded coconut
0.25 cup chopped almonds
1 beaten egg
0.3 cup low-fat milk
0.5 cup brown sugar
1 cup mashed banana
0.25 tsp salt
0.25 tsp baking soda
0.5 cup pumpkin pie spice
2 tsp baking powder
0.5 cup whole wheat flour
1 cup all-purpose flour

How to make:

1. Heat oven to 350°F. Spray oil on a loaf pan.
2. Mix salt, baking soda, pumpkin pie spice, baking powder, and both flours together. Blend oil, egg, milk, sugar, and bananas. Mix all ingredients; batter will be somewhat lumpy. Pour into the loaf pan and sprinkle on coconut and nuts. Bake 45-50 minutes, then let it cool.

Nutrition info per one slice:

150 calories
5 g fat (1 g saturated)
2 g fiber
25 g carbohydrates
3 g protein

11 g sugar
170 mg sodium

Feta and Onion Scones

Prep time: 20 mins
Bake time: 15 mins
Serves 12

Ingredients:

5 cups buttermilk
4 oz feta cheese
1 beaten egg
0.25 tsp pepper
0.25 tsp salt
0.25 tsp baking soda
2 tsp baking powder
2 tbsp finely chopped scallions
2 cups all-purpose flour

How to make:

1. Heat oven to 400°F. Mix flour, pepper, salt, baking soda, baking powder, and scallions, then blend well the buttermilk, cheese, and egg. Add the wet mix to the dry ingredients and stir gently.
2. Place dough on floured surface and knead 10 times. Cut dough in half, then roll each half in a 5-inch circle and cut each in six wedges. Put wedges on baking sheet and bake 15-18 minutes.

Nutrition info per scone:

106 calories
3 g fat (2 g saturated)
1 g fiber
15 g carbohydrates
5 g protein
1 g sugar

193 mg sodium

Vegan Cornbread

Prep time: 10 mins
Bake time: 35 mins
Serves 9

Ingredients:

3 tbsp oil
0.75 cup low-fat milk
0.5 tsp salt
1 tsp baking powder
2 tbsp sugar
0.75 cup whole wheat flour
1.25 cups cornmeal
2 tbsp flaxseed meal
5 tbsp water

How to make:

1. Heat oven to 350°F. Spray oil on an 8-inch baking pan.
2. Mix all the dry ingredients together. Blend flaxseed meal and water, then add oil and milk in it, then stir the flaxseed mix into the dry ingredients.
3. Pour mix into baking pan and bake for 25-30 minutes.

Nutrition info per slice:

168 calories
6 g fat (1 g saturated)
3 g fiber
25 g carbohydrates
4 g proteins
4 g sugar
201 mg sodium

Tomato Artichoke Focaccia

Prep time: 30 mins
Ready in: 2 hours and 35 mins
Serves 12

Ingredients:

4 cloves slivered garlic
1 small thinly sliced red onion
1 tbsp dried rosemary
1 tbsp oil
14-oz can artichoke hearts, drained and quartered
1.25 lbs. roma tomatoes
0.25 cup cornmeal
2 tbsp oil
1.25 cup warm water 120-130°F
1 tsp salt,
1 package active dry yeast
3.5-4 cups all-purpose flour

How to make:

1. Use large bowl to mix 1.5 cups flour, salt, and yeast. Add two tablespoons of oil and warm water. Beat high for 3 minutes, then mix in the cornmeal and as much flour as possible until dough becomes stiff. Put dough on floured surface. Use leftover flour to knead dough for 3-5 minutes. Form dough ball, then put it in a lightly greased bowl. Cover with clean towel and let the dough rise for 1 hour until twice its original size. Deflate and let it rest for 10 minutes.
2. Spray oil on an 11-inch by 13-inch baking dish. Place dough in it, pushing and stretching until dough fills the pan. Let rise for another 30 minutes.
3. Heat oven to 450°F. Lay artichoke pieces and tomato slices on top of the stretched dough, then sprinkle onion rings and garlic pieces. Bake for 25 minutes.

Nutrition info per slice:

148 calories
3 g fat (0 g saturated)
2 g fiber
26 g carbohydrates
4 g protein
2 g sugar
232 mg sodium

Rhubarb Oat Muffins

Prep time: 20 mins
Bake time: 25 mins
Serves 12

Ingredients:

0.25 cup chopped walnuts
0.5 tsp cinnamon
1 tbsp brown sugar
1 cup finely chopped rhubarb
2 tsp vanilla
2 tbsp oil
2 beaten eggs
0.75 cup buttermilk
0.25 tsp salt
0.5 tsp baking soda
1 tsp baking powder
0.5 cup pack brown sugar
0.5 cup all-purpose flour
0.75 cup whole wheat flour
1.75 cup oats
Spray oil

How to make:

1. Make streusel topping by mixing brown sugar, cinnamon, walnuts, and 0.25 cup of oats, then set aside.
2. Heat oven to 350°F. Put paper cups in a twelve-cup muffin pan.
3. Cream together the liquid ingredients and stir in rhubarb. In another bowl, mix all the dry ingredients, then add in the cream mix. Spoon into muffin pan and garnish with streusel topping. Bake for 20-22 minutes.

Nutrition info per muffin:

181 calories
5 g fat (1 g saturated)
3 g fiber
30 g carbohydrates
5 g protein
11 g sugar
180 mg sodium

Sesame Cheese Twists

Prep time: 15 mins
Bake time: 15 mins
Makes 36

Ingredients:

1 tbsp sesame seeds
1 tsp paprika
2 tbsp skim milk
1 egg + 1 for egg wash
3 tbsp grated Parmesan cheese
2 tbsp light margarine
0.25 tsp salt
0.75 cup white flour
0.75 cup wheat flour

How to make:

1. Heat oven to 350°F. Sift all the dry ingredients into a bowl.
   Add margarine and cut in, then add the parmesan cheese.
   Beat the milk and egg in a separate bowl. Mix all ingredients
   together until a dough forms.
2. Knead dough on floured surface for 2 minutes. Roll dough
   into square and brush with egg wash. Sprinkle on paprika and
   sesame seeds. Cut dough into 0.5-inch strips, twist slightly,
   and lay on baking pan. Bake for 15 minutes.

Nutrition info per two sticks:

53 calories
2 g fat (0 sat)
8 g carbohydrates
1 g fiber
0 g sugar
2 g protein

Lemon Bread

Prep time: 10 mins
Bake time: 40 mins
Serves 10

Ingredients:

1.5 tsp lemon zest
0.5 cup low-fat milk
0.5 tsp salt
1 tsp baking powder
1.5 cups flour
0.5 cup beaten egg whites
0.5 cup room temperature margarine
1 cup sugar substitute

How to make:

1. Heat oven to 350°F. Spray oil on a loaf-shaped baking pan.
2. Mix all ingredients until smooth. Pour into the baking pan and bake for 45-50 minutes.

Nutrition info per slice:

157 calories
4 g protein
1 g fat (0 sat)
15 g carbohydrates
7 g fiber
230 mg sodium

Sour Cream Potato Biscuits

Prep time: 15 mins
Bake time: 15 mins
Makes 15

Ingredients:

0.5 tsp baking soda, 0.5 tsp
1 tsp salt
1 tbsp baking powder
1.75 cups flour
2 tbsp butter
0.25 cup low-fat sour cream
0.5 cup low-fat buttermilk
8 oz cooked and mashed Yukon gold potatoes

How to make:

1. Heat oven to 450°F. Cream together the butter, sour cream, and potatoes. Add in the dry ingredients and mix well. Add buttermilk and form a dough ball.
2. Put ball on floured surface and roll to ¾-inch thick. Cut out biscuits and put on a baking pan. Bake 15 minutes.

Nutrition info per biscuit:

87 calories
2.2 g fat (1.3 g saturated)
2.2 g protein
14.5 g carbohydrates
0.6 g fiber
298 mg sodium

Cheddar Biscuits

Prep time: 15 mins
Bake time: 15 mins
Makes 8

Ingredients:

0.66 cup fat-free milk
0.25 cup shredded low-fat cheddar cheese
1 tbsp oil
2 tbsp fat-free plain Greek yogurt
2 tbsp cubed butter
0.25 tsp salt
2 tsp baking powder
1.75 cups flour

How to make:

1. Heat oven to 425°F. Spray oil on a flat baking pan.
2. Mix baking powder, salt, and flour. Cut into dry ingredients the oil, yogurt, and butter. Add in cheese, then pour in milk and make a dough ball.
3. Knead the dough on a floured counter 10 times. Roll dough to 0.5-inch thick. Cut out biscuits and bake 15 minutes.

Nutrition info per biscuit:

159 calories
6 g fat (3 g saturated)
1 g fiber
22 g carbohydrates
5 g protein
1 g sugar
253 mg sodium

Pizza Crust

Prep time: 10 mins
Bake time: 15 mins
Serves 8

Ingredients:

0.5 tsp salt
2 tbsp cream cheese
2 cups shredded mozzarella cheese
0.75 cup almond flour

How to make:

1. Heat oven to 425°F. Pour all the ingredients in a saucepan. Use low heat to warm, stir continuously until cheese melts.
2. Set dough ball on a parchment paper and lay another sheet on top. Roll in 12-inch round shape. Lay dough on pizza pan using one sheet of parchment paper. Make holes in the dough with tines of fork. Bake for 6 minutes, then allow to cool before putting in the desired toppings. Bake pizza for 8 minutes.

Chapter 8: Snacks

Sometimes, we just need a nice snack to tide us over until the next meal or a little something to relax with before bedtime. The following are some healthy snack options anyone in the family can enjoy:

1. Celery sticks with peanut butter
2. Edamame
3. Trail mix
4. Popcorn
5. Whole grain crackers with cheese
6. Cottage cheese
7. Turkey and sliced cheese rolls
8. Apple slices with peanut butter
9. Avocado
10. Hummus with veggie sticks
11. Almonds
12. Yogurt and berries
13. Hardboiled eggs
14. Low-sodium soup
15. Berry smoothie

Chapter 9: Sample Menus

Here are sample menus for the first week of healthy eating in which the recipes can be found in this cookbook. Remember, these are sample suggestions, so feel free to mix and match to create your own delicious menu choices. And, yes, dessert is included!

Day One
Breakfast: Vegetable Quiche
Lunch: Turkey Reuben
Dinner: Cod with Tomato Sauce
Dessert: Banana Oat Bars

Day Two
Breakfast: Breakfast Parfait
Lunch: Thai Chicken Lettuce Wraps
Dinner: Ham Soup
Dessert: Chocolate Cream Delight

Day Three
Breakfast: Ham Egg Pitas
Lunch: Chicken and Egg Salad
Dinner: Vegetarian Chili
Dessert: Lemon Pound Cake

Day Four
Breakfast: Turkey Bacon Muffins
Lunch: Ham and Fruit Salad
Dinner: Mushroom Beef Skillet
Dessert: Almond Cheesecake Bars

Day Five
Breakfast: Banana Nut Oatmeal
Lunch: Spinach Rolls
Dinner: Cranberry Mustard Pork Medallions
Dessert: Baked Apples

Day Six
Breakfast: Breakfast Smoothie
Lunch: Salmon Couscous Salad
Dinner: Asian Pork Chops
Dessert: Gingerbread Biscotti

Day 7
Breakfast: Southwest Scramble
Lunch: Roast Beef Pita
Dinner: Baked Fish and Veggies
Dessert: Chocolate Brownies

Conclusion

Thank you for making it through to the end of *Diabetes Type 2 Cookbook: Great, Healthy, Delicious Recipes for Diabetics* by Sierra A. May. Let's hope it was informative and able to provide you with all of the tools you need to achieve your goals whatever they may be.

The next step is to use the sample menus to get started on your weight loss journey in the best tasting way possible. Use all of the recipes in this book, in as many combinations as you can think of, and enjoy good eating while working toward your goal of a healthy lifestyle.

Finally, if you found this book useful in any way, a review on Amazon is always appreciated!

Connect with us on our Facebook page

www.facebook.com/bluesourceandfriends and stay tuned to our

latest book promotions and free giveaways.

Sierra A. May

Printed in Great Britain
by Amazon

51622327R00072